THINGS YOU SHOULD KNOW ABOUT

Whales & Dolphins

By Steve Parker

Illustrated by
Syd Brak

BYEWAY
B O O K S

First published in 2003 by
Miles Kelly Publishing Ltd
Bardfield Centre
Great Bardfield
Essex, CM7 4SL

This 2005 edition published by Byeway Books
Byeway Books Inc.
Lenexa, KS 66219, 866-4BYEWAY
www.byewaybooks.com

Editorial Director: Belinda Gallagher
Editorial Assistant: Lisa Clayden
Designer: Herring Bone Design
Artwork Commissioner: Bethany Walker
Production: Estela Boulton, Elizabeth Brunwin
Indexer: Jane Parker

Library of Congress Cataloging-in-Publication
Data is on file at the Library of Congress.

ISBN 1-933581-26-3

Printed in China

2 4 6 8 10 9 7 5 3 1

Contents

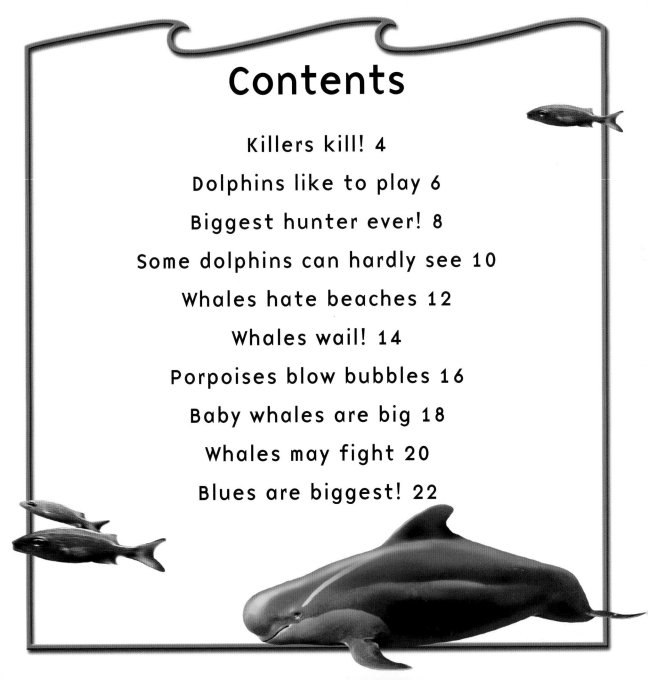

1 Killers kill!

Dolphin facts

- Killer "whales" are really the largest members of the dolphin group.
- A big male is about 33 ft (10 m) long and weighs 10 tons.
- Killer whales roam all seas, although they rarely visit the warmest tropics.
- Killer whales are also called orcas.

All whales and dolphins feed on other animals. The **KILLER WHALE** hunts big prey such as seals, albatrosses, and fish as large as you. But sometimes the killer whale makes do with a small fish as a snack.

Killer whales "talk" in clicks and squeaks as they circle their prey.

Wave of death

Some killer whales ride the surf onto the beach, grab a seal, and wriggle back into the sea to eat it.

Killer whales live in groups called pods. The older females are in charge. Their offspring (young) may stay together for 10 to 20 years.

The tall fin on the back is called the dorsal fin. It helps the killer whale to swim straight, without tilting over.

The killer has about 50 teeth, each one almost as big as your hand. They are suited for grabbing and tearing, not chewing.

These massive mammals can swim along at 30 m/h (50 km/h).

2 Dolphins like to play

Dolphins often leap from the water and fall back with a splash and crash—because they want to! They seem to play and have fun. But their play could be partly serious. Perhaps these **BOTTLENOSE DOLPHINS** want to attract a partner for breeding. Or they make noise to gather fish into a small area—for dinner!

Dolphin facts
• The bottlenose dolphin grows to about 13 ft (4 m) long.
• It lives in warmer oceans worldwide.
• It sometimes gathers in huge schools (groups) of over 500.

The dolphin's snout, or beak, is shaped like a round, hard bottle. In its mouth are 100 small, sharp teeth, ready to snap up a meal.

A dolphin's smooth, slippery skin slides through the water at super speed. The bottlenose dolphin races along at 30 m/h (50 km/h)— far faster than a person can run.

Click-click

Dolphins click and squeak, and can hear these sounds bounce back off fish. This is how they find dinner in muddy water or at night.

The dolphin waves its tail flukes (fins) up and down with great power, to get up to top speed.

Bottlenose dolphins can leap more than 20 ft (6 m) out of the water. But they need a good "run-up." They dive down deep, then swim upwards fast, bursting from the surface in a fountain of spray.

Biggest hunter ever!

Whale facts

- Sperm whales live in all oceans, even cold polar waters.
- The bull (male) grows to about 66 ft (20 m) long and 50 tons in weight.
- The cow (female) is about 49 ft (15 m) long and half as heavy.

Great meat-eating dinosaurs like *Tyrannosaurus* were huge, but the **SPERM WHALE** is ten times bigger—the largest hunter that has ever lived. It is also one of the deepest divers in the whale group, heading down over thousands of feet into the ocean depths.

This huge whale has a huge appetite. It hunts big fish, octopus, and even the dreaded giant squid.

Sperm whales can hold their breath for more than one hour, as they dive down and down. They use clicks of sound, which they hear bouncing back off nearby objects, to find their prey in the darkness.

The sperm whale's back fin is just a small hump, with even smaller humps behind.

There are about 50 cone-shaped teeth in the very narrow lower jaw—but no teeth at all in the upper jaw.

Small giants!

There are three kinds of sperm whale. The pygmy one is medium-sized. The dwarf sperm whale is "tiny" yet still twice as big as a person!

4 Some dolphins can hardly see

Dolphin facts

- The susu grows to more than 8 ft (2.5 m) in length.
- It weighs up to 198 lb (90 kg).
- Female susus are slightly larger than males.
- Another local name for this dolphin is the bhulan.

There are about 38 kinds of dolphins. But only five types live all their lives in fresh water, in rivers and lakes. The **SUSU**, also known as the Ganges River dolphin, is from the Indian region. It is very shy and extremely endangered.

Like all whales and dolphins, the susu's flippers are paddle-shaped for swimming and steering.

The susu comes up for air often, every minute or two.

Whales and dolphins swim by arching the body to swish the tail flukes up and down (fish have upright tail fins and bend their bodies from side to side).

Safe or not?
Most sharks have triangular fins, while most dolphins have swept-back ones.

The susu has tiny, deep-set eyes. These can only pick out blurs of light and darkness. The dolphin finds its way mainly by sound clicks.

Susus have more than 120 small, sharp teeth. They work like spikes to grab fish, shellfish, worms, and crabs, near the riverbed and in the mud.

Whales hate beaches

Dolphin facts

- Pilot whales live in all oceans except for the far north and south.
- Males are up to 23 ft (7 m) long and 2 tons in weight.
- Females are smaller, but live longer—up to 60 years.

PILOT WHALES, like most whales and dolphins, usually stay away from the shore. But sometimes they follow prey into the shallows. Then they are in danger of being stranded—stuck on the beach, where they would soon die.

Pilot "whales" are really large dolphins. They are also called "blackfish."

The forehead is very rounded, or bulbous, giving the nickname "melon-head."

Stick to mother

A baby whale or dolphin is called a calf. It feeds on its mother's milk and stays near her all the time. A new baby pilot whale is 5 ft (1.6 m) long.

Pilot whales usually hunt in deep water, diving down 1,600 ft or more. They hold their breath for over 15 minutes as they chase squid, octopus, and fish.

Pilot whales live in groups called schools, which can number over 100. Sometimes they swim with other dolphins, or perhaps with small whales such as minkes.

Each pilot whale in the group makes its own special clicks and whistles, which the others recognize.

If one pilot whale is ill or injured, the others gather round. They try to protect and look after it.

6 Whales wail!

Whale facts

- The humpback is one of the bigger whales, about 50 ft (15 m) long and weighing up to 40 tons.
- It lives in all the world's oceans.
- Humpbacks migrate to colder waters in summer, and back to warmer regions for winter.

All whales and dolphins make clicks, squeaks, squeals, moans, wails, and other sounds. These travel fast and far through the water. The male **HUMPBACK WHALE** is one of the champion singers. He is probably trying to attract a female with his loud, long "love-song."

Humpbacks have lots of lumps and bumps on their heads. Hard-shelled sea creatures called barnacles also live there.

As the humpback sings, he arches his body so that his head and tail droop downwards. He does not swim, but hangs in mid-water.

The song lasts for 40 minutes or more. Then the humpback sings it all again—and again, for up to 20 hours!

Each male has his own song. It carries huge distances through the ocean—62 miles (100 km) or more. Also, he changes it slightly from one year to the next.

The humpback's flippers are massive, up to 16 ft (5 m) long, with lumps along the front edge.

Mouthful of sea
The humpback gulps a vast mouthful of water and squeezes it out again, trapping small animals inside for its food.

Porpoises blow bubbles

The **HARBOR PORPOISE** is a close cousin of whales and dolphins. Like them, and us, it is a mammal. This means it has warm blood and it breathes air. But its nose is not at the front of the face—it's on the top of the head! This breathing opening is called a blowhole.

All porpoises, whales, and dolphins hold their breath under the water, although a few bubbles of air may escape from the blowhole.

Porpoise facts

- There are six kinds of porpoises around the world.
- The harbor porpoise is about 5.5 ft (1.7 m) long and 143 lb (65 kg) in weight.

As its name suggests, the harbor porpoise sometimes comes into ports and harbors, especially at night. It noses about among the rubbish on the seabed, for bits of old fish and other scraps that people throw away.

The harbor porpoise usually hunts alone in shallow waters near the shore. It feasts mainly on fish and shellfish.

Lots of teeth

Dolphins and porpoises have many small, sharp teeth for spiking slippery fish and stabbing squirming squid.

When these animals return to the surface, they blow out the stale air, making a spray that looks like a fountain!

Baby whales are big

Whale facts

- A full-grown gray whale is 49 ft (15 m) long and 35 tons in weight.
- Gray whales live along the coasts of the North Pacific Ocean.

Just like other mammals, whale and dolphin mothers give birth to babies and feed them on milk. The newborn **GRAY WHALE** is one of the world's biggest babies— 16 ft (5 m) long and weighing half a ton!

The mother whale's teats are on her rear underside, towards her tail. She lies on her side so her baby can breathe easily while it is feeding.

The mother gray whale is pregnant (when her baby is growing inside her womb) for 13 months.

The baby whale sometimes partly lies on its mother, for a rest or a piggy-back ride. The mother helps it to reach the surface regularly, for breaths of fresh air.

Pesky pests

A whale is like a moving rock, where barnacles, limpets and other creatures attach themselves and grow.

The young whale, or calf, depends on its mother for milk and protection for 9 months. Then it is old enough to fend for itself.

whales may fight

Whale facts

• Narwhals live in the far north, among the icebergs of the Arctic Ocean.
• A narwhal is about 15 ft (4.5 m) long and weighs 1.5 tons.

In some types of whales, the males fight each other at breeding time. Male **NARWHALS** show off their long tusks, waving them in the air at each other, and even using them like swords in a fencing fight.

The male that wins the contest is most likely to mate with a female and become a father. However he does not take any care of the baby. Only female whales and dolphins care for their young.

The narwhal's tusk is not used for eating.
These whales feed by powerfully sucking in small animals, with their bendy lips and tongue.

The narwhal's corkscrew-like tusk is a very long, sharp tooth called an incisor. It grows from the upper jaw, out through the skin, and up to 10 ft (3 m) long. Usually only the male has the tusk.

Whitest whale
The narwhal's close cousin in far-north waters is the beluga. It is all-white, and is also the noisiest whale—and it can make faces!

Narwhals eat many kinds of fish and shellfish, especially from the seabed. They also make a wide range of loud noises that can even be heard above the surface.

21

Blues are biggest!

Whale facts

- The blue whale is a true giant, almost 98 ft (30 m) long and 150 tons in weight.
- It lives in all the world's oceans.
- Blues swim to the far north or south for summer, and back to the tropics for winter.

The **BLUE WHALE** is the largest creature in the world. Yet its main food, the shrimplike shellfish called krill, are each smaller than your finger. The blue whale eats more than one million of them every day.

Great whales such as the blue whale have no teeth. Their mouths contain long strips of a tough, springy substance called baleen or "whalebone."

When people hunted blue whales, they became very rare. Now these great whales are protected by laws. They are slowly increasing their numbers again.

But many small whales, dolphins and porpoises are still hunted. Others are trapped in fishing nets and drown, or they are poisoned by pollution. All of these amazing sea mammals need our care and protection.

Whale out of water

It is hard to imagine how big a blue whale is, unless you lift it out of the water and take it home—which would be quite difficult!

The blue whale opens its mouth wide, takes a gulp of water and krill, then closes its mouth to squeeze out the water through its baleen. The brush-edged strips work like a massive comb, to filter the water and trap the krill inside. The whale then licks off the krill and swallows them.

Index